# ZEN STORIES OF THE SAMURAI

Pádric,

Great training with you

Thank you for the wonderful Hospitality

Neal Dumuga
June 9, 2016

# ZEN STORIES OF THE SAMURAI

### By Neal Dunnigan
#### Drawings by John Hrabushi

#### Foreword by Lorraine DiAnne, Shihan

Global Thinking Books
Kingfisher, Oklahoma

# ZEN STORIES OF THE SAMURAI

www.zenstoriesofthesamurai.com

Copyright:

© Global Thinking, Inc., 2004 All rights reserved.

Brief quotations may be printed in critical articles and reviews. All other reproduction, archiving, broadcast, and performance is prohibited without the prior written permission of **Global Thinking, Inc.**

Published by:

Lulu Enterprises, Inc.
Morrisville, NC 27560

While every precaution has been taken in the preparation of this book, the publisher assumes no responsibilities for errors or omissions, or for damages resulting from the use of information contained herein.

This book would not have been possible without:

- Zen masters and martial artists of ancient times, who discovered the way;
- Their successors, who refined and passed on their discoveries;
- Contemporary scholars and masters, who disseminated that knowledge around the world;
- My many fine teachers;
- My family.

Dedicated to my beloved wife, Virginia Giglio.

*Zen Stories of the Samurai*

# Table of Contents

Foreword ......................................................................... x

Preface .......................................................................... xiii

Introduction ................................................................. 20

Teachers and Disciples.................................................. 30
   Preparing for Training.................................................. 31
   Understanding the Teaching...................................... 35
   Searching for a Successor.......................................... 37
   Learning from the Penitent........................................ 39

Insights ......................................................................... 42
   Trusting Intuition....................................................... 43
   Perceiving Mastery.................................................... 45
   Releasing the Mind.................................................... 47
   Discerning Intentions ................................................ 48

Monk Encounters........................................................... 52
   Knowing and Not-Knowing ........................................ 53
   Penetrating Defenses ................................................ 55
   Sustaining Concentration .......................................... 57
   Meaning and Mind..................................................... 59
   Unblocking the Imagination....................................... 60
   Moving Freely............................................................ 62
   Understanding by Being............................................. 65

Kenchoji Temple ........................................................... 68
   Going Beyond the Ordinary ....................................... 69
   Puzzling Achievement................................................ 71
   Clearing Confusion .................................................... 72
   Making Jizo Stand ..................................................... 74
   Underestimating Loyalty ........................................... 76
   Persevering to the End ............................................. 78

High and Mighty............................................................ 81
   Cutting Off Fear........................................................ 82
   Reevaluating the Beautiful ........................................ 85
   Testing for Worthiness............................................... 87
   Commanding the Elusive ........................................... 89
   Reprimanding Arrogance............................................ 92
   Acting Nobly.............................................................. 94
   Seizing the Moment .................................................. 95
   Approaching the Formidable....................................... 97
   Dispelling Illusions .................................................... 101
   Inventing Success...................................................... 103

Riff Raff ........................................................................ 106
   Exposing the Bully .................................................... 107

## Table of Contents

Acting Spontaneously .............................................110
Transferring Mastery.............................................113

*Imminent Death* .................................................*118*
Viewing the World ...............................................119
Accepting Reality................................................120
Living with Death ...............................................123

*About the Illustrations*........................................*124*

*About the Authors*..............................................*129*

*Bibliography*...................................................*130*

*Index* .........................................................*133*

# Foreword

I was introduced to Zen stories by my first Aikido instructor. In addition to being an Aikido sensei, he was also a philosophy professor at Smith College. During the course of our Aikido training sessions, he would periodically interject a Zen story. Looking back, I cannot say that either my training partners or I always "got" the connection between those stories and our martial arts training. Nevertheless, these stories did have an impact on my thinking at that time. If nothing else, those Zen stories reinforced my intellectual curiosity and encouraged me to consider the validity of rejecting the assumed premise and accepting alternative ways of viewing problems.

Later on, when I continued my martial arts studies in Japan, I found myself immersed in a culture where this type of story was thoroughly enmeshed into the fabric of daily life. In Japan, Zen stories played a significant role in passing on cultural heritage and philosophical knowledge, both for martial arts and for society in general.

When I returned to the United States, I kept up with my study of Japanese culture along with my pursuit of the martial arts. In my various readings, again I encountered Zen stories; this time with a difference relevance.

Neal Dunnigan became my Aikido student over a decade ago. When he first made me aware of his plans for this project, I

### Zen Stories of the Samurai

wondered: Why a book? Why Neal? Why now? After I had the opportunity to review one of the early manuscript drafts, it became clear to me. The collection, itself, reflects a perfect wholeness. The stories are simple, direct, easy to read, and have completeness in their scope. Neal Dunnigan has expressed these stories in a style that is relevant and accessible to the contemporary American martial artist. The illustrations by John Hrabushi are excellent and capture the essence of the stories.

I recommend this book to martial arts students at all levels. In my experience, it is more likely that martial arts training will help the readers to understand the stories, than it is that these stories will help the reader understand the martial arts. At the most basic level, these stories will give the reader important insights into Japanese culture and history. More significantly, these stories have the potential to help martial arts students better integrate their martial arts training into their everyday lives. If martial arts students were to read and reflect, over and over, on these stories with an open heart, these stories could well help take them wherever they want to go.

Lorraine DiAnne, Shihan

November 2004

# Preface

This is a book for martial arts students and others who are looking for an insight into the influence of Zen Buddhism on the martial arts of feudal Japan. It may also serve as useful supplementary material for those readers looking for an introduction to Zen Buddhism from a martial arts perspective.

I first became interested in martial arts when I was a student at a Catholic high school. The religious component of our curriculum included the study of Christian doctrine and comparative religions as well. We spent a portion of one semester studying Buddhism. I don't know how much understanding our class absorbed. I do remember that I was inexplicably intrigued by the stories I read that depicted encounters between Japanese samurai and Zen masters.

I found the paradoxical and enigmatic dialogs between the samurai and Zen masters intellectually and emotionally absorbing. To an uninitiated reader, they made little or no sense. They appeared to be either trivial or nonsensical. The samurai in the stories did not appear particularly religious, at least not in any sense that I had known. In fact, the samurai preoccupation with the arts of killing appeared contrary to what little I thought I knew of Buddhism. One thing that I could understand was that something about Zen had seriously captured these warriors' interests.

## Preface

After a while, my initial attempts to fathom these stories left me intellectually exhausted. I began to suspect that the meaning of the stories transcended the literal text of their puzzling dialogues. Perhaps the stories themselves had no intrinsic meaning and were only pointers to experiential truths. I resolved that given the opportunity, I would try to understand these stories experientially by pursuing the martial arts.

That philosophical challenge was the beginning of my lifelong pursuit of martial arts.

My purpose in assembling this collection is to introduce these stories to a new generation of readers, with a special focus on the contemporary western martial artist. Short stories, poems, and anecdotes are common teaching tools in Zen Buddhism. From that large body of literature, this collection focuses exclusively on martial stories, typically depicting Zen encounters by samurai warriors of feudal Japan.

In building this story collection, I made certain editorial decisions to unify the historical, philosophical, and linguistic aspects of the collection.

A few of the stories are older Chinese stories that have long been adapted and adopted by the Japanese. In these cases, I have used names and terminology associated with the Japanese versions. This preference is not a political statement; it is merely a convenience

xiv

## Zen Stories of the Samurai

for the reader in order to make the overall style of the collection more consistent.

Many of the stories in the collection are associated with historical figures. The actual events depicted, however, are often apocryphal. In collecting and retelling these stories, I have taken the approach that it is not so important whether the stories are literally true, but rather that the stories accurately communicate a truth. The value of these stories lies in the thoughts that they invoke in the reader, not in the historical knowledge that they impart. Readers interested in the deeper historical aspects of these stories should consult the sources listed in the Bibliography.

The majority of these stories can be considered folklore. The wordings are not directly based on any particular literal Japanese translation. Rather, a contemporary, American English, free translation is used to communicate more clearly the original intent of the stories. Some of these stories do have authoritative, Japanese language, original sources (e.g., temple records) and some do not. Those stories where "official" Japanese versions do exist are typically written in an archaic form of Japanese no longer in common use. This evolution in Japanese language usage is somewhat analogous to the difference in style between Elizabethan English and contemporary American English.

These problems created by the semantic and style differences between modern and earlier Japanese language usage are compounded by some of the available English translations. While some of the standard reference translations are quite accurate in a

## Preface

scholarly sense, they have an early 20th century literary style that contemporary readers might find awkward and therefore less accessible. Some of these earlier translations are parts of larger historical or theological works that may deter the casual reader because of their size or academic orientation.

In addition to applying a unified style, I have made other attempts to render the material more accessible to the novice reader. Instead of using diacritic markings, this text uses only standard North American alphabet characters. For the purposes of this collection, the slight pronunciation assistance the diacritic markings might provide is less significant than the potential distraction they cause for the novice reader. For example, the name *Yagyu* is used in place of *Yagyū*.

In these stories, I have avoided any Japanese terminology other than names of people and locations. Proper names often have alternative English spellings. In these situations, the more common English spelling is used. For example, the warlord of Uchigo province is referred to as *Uesugi Kenshin* rather than as *Uyesugi Kenshin*.

Where translated words have replaced Japanese terminology, the English words are commonly used approximations rather than literal translations. Some of the previously published versions of these stories include un-translated Japanese political and cultural terminology. While this terminology is both succinct and intellectually enriching, it does potentially distract the uninitiated reader from the point of the story. Therefore, I have avoided that

## Zen Stories of the Samurai

practice in this collection. For example, *warlord* is used for the Japanese term *daimyo*, *saint* is used for the Japanese term *bodhisattva*, and *Zen Master* is used for the Japanese term *Roshi*. Only three untranslated Japanese terms are used: *samurai* (a member of the warrior class), *Zen* (a sect of Buddhism), and *Shogun* (the hereditary military dictator of feudal Japan).

Some Japanese terms, especially philosophical terms, have no direct English translation. For a novice reader, that problem is a potential intellectual roadblock. In other books that give these stories a more scholarly treatment, the explanations for these terms often involve tracing their etymologies back to their Chinese origins and then even further back to their Sanskrit origins. In this collection, I have attempted to express the purposeful intent of each story entirely within the context itself, rather than introduce additional terminology that would require yet further definition. While arcane terminology is avoided here, I encourage interested readers to delve more deeply into terminology with the use of scholarly resources such as D. T. Suzuki (see Bibliography).

Although they share a Buddhist foundation, these stories are not inherently religious. The attraction of the samurai to Zen was arguably as much a matter of expediency as it was one of theology. These stories deal not with deities, but rather with the nature of immediacy and its role in understanding the essence of the human existence. The reader needs no particular religious background to appreciate these stories. This collection is not in any way intended to proselytize the reader toward or away from Zen in particular or Buddhism in general. Those readers looking for a

xvii

## Preface

deeper insight into Zen or other aspects of Buddhism may be interested in several of the works cited in the Bibliography. For those readers who are interested in the comparative religious aspects of Zen and Christianity, the works of Thomas Merton, cited in the Bibliography, can provide additional reading.

This collection, while small and attractively illustrated, is not easy on the reader. Understanding Zen concepts may be beyond the reach of many contemporary American martial arts students. The stories are challenging. While they appear simple, comprehending them requires deep reflection. I recommend that the reader pick up the book many times, reading only one or two stories per sitting. After a reading, take the time to reflect on the story. Consider each story both from the context of the story's original setting and also from the perspective of your life at the moment.

The drawings that separate the chapters are provided as a kind of mental speed bump. They provide an opportunity to stop and reflect. Occasionally humorous, but always profound, John Hrabushi's drawings offer the reader a kind of meditative "cross training" that will enhance the appreciation of the stories. For those not familiar with this style of art, a brief explanation of Zen ink painting is provided along with a short description of each drawing (see About the Illustrations.)

Although I have reflected on these stories for over 30 years, I am neither a master nor a teacher of Buddhism. Any errors in this collection are mine alone.

My hope is that the readers will find themselves intrigued by these stories and illustrations. Beyond that, I hope that this collection will inspire readers to apply themselves more diligently to their intellectual and physical training and their own personal quest for spiritual discipline.

# Introduction

The Japanese term *zen* refers to meditation. It also is the term associated with a well-known movement in Buddhism, which happens to encourage the practice of meditation as one of its central principles.

The study of Zen Buddhism, or simply Zen, is a process that has occupied the entire lives of various scholars and saints. At the risk of great oversimplification, Zen as practiced in feudal Japan can be bounded by the following working definition:

> A family of related denominations of Mahayana (i.e., northern) Buddhism, which in feudal Japan included the Rinzai, Soto, and Obaku sects. These sects are characterized by:
>
> - A focus on enlightenment through sudden and intuitive self-awareness rather than ritual, ethical, or intellectual endeavors;
> - An emphasis on the practice of meditation;
> - The rejection of theological and philosophical abstraction, speculation, and conceptualization.

Within the culture of feudal Japan, Zen was as much a social and philosophical phenomenon as it was a religion. Zen provided the Japanese with a way of looking at life and living that the Japanese

**Zen Stories of the Samurai**

people carried over into many secular activities. These included archery, fencing, flower arranging, landscaping, painting, poetry, puppetry, tea ceremony, and theater. Even to the present day, the Zen-influenced schools of these arts are still flourishing. In fact, the practice of these arts, with a Zen perspective, has been adopted by people of many different religious faiths all around the world.

The origin of Zen goes back to the 5th century when Buddhist missionaries from India arrived in China. According to tradition, the most notable of these missionaries was Bodhidharma (better known in Japan as Bodai Daruma or simply Daruma). Bodai Daruma traveled to northern China where he took up residence at the Shaolin monastery that had already been established by earlier Buddhist missionaries. As the new leader of the Shaolin community, Bodai Daruma instituted a number of reforms. One of these reforms was to place a greater emphasis on the practice of meditation. Allegedly, Bodai Daruma realized that many of the Shaolin monks did not have the physical or mental stamina to withstand his intense approach to meditation. As a result, Bodai Daruma introduced a series of yoga-like exercises to strengthen and discipline the monks. These exercises eventually developed into Chinese Kung-fu and the first connection between Zen and martial arts was established.

Zen (called Chan by the Chinese) along with other Buddhist sects continued to gain in popularity in China where they coexisted with the indigenous Taoist and Confucian schools of thought.

## Introduction

Buddhism was first introduced to Japan from Korea during the 6th century. Within a few generations, Japanese Prince Shotoku had elevated Buddhism's status by his official patronage. Buddhism soon displaced Shinto as Japan's official state religion. By the 9th century, several non-Zen sects of Buddhism had become well established in Japan and were coexisting along with Japan's indigenous Shinto religion. By the time Zen Buddhism arrived in Japan, these religious predecessors had already made their marks on Japanese martial arts.

In the earliest portion of Japan's recorded history, the Shinto tradition established martial arts both as an integral part of the Japanese creation myth and as a symbol of the divine providence of the Japanese imperial family. By Japan's feudal period (552 – 1868), some martial arts schools also attributed their establishment to similar divine providence. Tradition claims that the founders of these schools received divine instruction from spirit beings associated with Shinto beliefs. Even in contemporary Japan, the ceremonial process for forging swords is still accompanied by Shinto purification rituals.

Among the non-Zen Buddhist sects in feudal Japan, the Tendai and Shingon sects in particular were known for large monasteries staffed with warrior monks. The martial training of monks made the Tendai and Shingon monasteries significant military and political forces in feudal Japan. The powerful Tendai and Shingon monasteries cultivated the study of various martial arts, particularly those related to the spear and other pole arms.

## Zen Stories of the Samurai

The introduction of Zen to Japan came in the 13th century. The Zen missionaries Dogen and Eisai are credited with bringing Zen from China and introducing it to Japan. This missionary work had the official support of the Japanese government, which hoped that the introduction of a new Buddhist sect would potentially dilute the social and economic power of the existing sects.

The 13th century was a turbulent time in Japanese history. The country was at risk of invasion from abroad and civil war at home. The power of government had long since been taken from the emperor and his imperial court, leaving them with only figurehead status. The actual political power was held by a hereditary military dictator called the Shogun who ruled in the emperor's name.

The Shogun's hold on power, however, was tentative. He depended on the support of warlords who controlled the provinces. These provincial warlords in turn depended on lesser warlords. This was a feudal system built on a pyramid of vassals serving superior lords. Taken together, all of these military officials, their soldiers, and their families, constituted a warrior class known as the samurai.

By the 13th century, Japan's samurai society had begun to evolve from class to caste, with the role of the warrior on its way to becoming an exclusively inherited one. Over time, the samurai became more distinct and isolated from other Japanese people by law, custom, clothing, hairstyle, and family lineage.

## Introduction

From the 13th century onward, Zen was readily adopted by many among Japan's samurai class. Certainly not all samurai became adherents to the Zen sects of Buddhism. However, the concepts of Zen Buddhism eventually influenced the thinking of the samurai in general. Those concepts also provided the framework to give Japanese martial arts a new perspective.

The word *samurai* is derived from a Japanese term meaning *one who serves*. The hallmarks of the samurai were their loyalty and absolute dedication to the service of their immediate lord. This responsibility was taken so seriously that a samurai would disregard his own personal safety, not only risking his life, but in some circumstances even deliberately taking his own life to serve his lord.

In our modern society, we can easily reference well-known examples of selfless acts of heroism (e.g., the fire fighters at the World Trade Center or Chernobyl disasters.) Even with these models in mind, it is still difficult for us to appreciate the extreme and pervasive nature of the feudal Japanese concepts of loyalty and honor as they blended into the samurai's unique concept of duty.

Perhaps that is because in our contemporary culture, we place a high value on calculated actions. We live in a world of outcome analysis, loss-to-benefit evaluations, and measured risk taking. To the samurai, our modern approach to risk taking would be abhorrent, particularly when dealing with matters of honor or service to one's feudal lord.

# Zen Stories of the Samurai

The mainstream nature of the samurai's intense abandonment of life and death is reflected in Yamamoto Tsunenori's essay providing guidance to young warriors.

The way of the warrior is death. This means choosing to die whenever there is a choice between life and death. It means nothing more then this. You must remain completely resolved to this. Truisms like, "To die with your intentions unrealized is to die uselessly" are merely weak-minded sophistry. People, who become unresolved as to whether to stay with their original plan when faced with a choice between life and death, have allowed their natural attachment to life get out of control. They let their desire for life warp the logic of their decision making. Accepting death without regard to success is not a shameful or foolish thing. It is the most important thing in the way of the warrior.

If you keep your heart in the right place from morning to night, staying accustomed to the idea of death, and being resolved on death, then you can consider yourself to have already become a dead body. Once you have done that, you will be one with the way of the warrior, and you can pass through life with no possibility of failure and perform your office.

- in *Hagakure,* 18th Century

## Introduction

From this example, we can see how the Japanese culture of that time was so acceptant of ritual suicide, a trait that we closely associate with the samurai.

More significantly, this excerpt explains how an over attachment to living, or a fear of dying, would be seen as impediments to samurai in the performance of their duties to their feudal lords. Not only did these attachments and fears have the potential to hinder a samurai's direct actions, but they also had the potential of corrupting a samurai's reasoning and weakening his underlying dedication.

This is the cultural case for the inherent affinity between samurai and Zen: the practice of Zen was able to free a samurai from attachment to life and death. Such a samurai would theoretically be a better vassal to his feudal lord and more capable of fulfilling his societal obligations.

These ideas were not without challenge. By the latter part of the Japanese feudal period, some Japanese samurai philosophers, like Chozan Shissai in the 18th century, criticized what they perceived as the nihilistic aspects of Zen. These thinkers saw greater utility in neo-Confucian principles that emphasized social responsibility based on social order.

Beyond the Zen cultural connection based on the samurai role as a vassal, another connection was based on the samurai role as a martial artist. This is a personal, rather than social, connection and

# Zen Stories of the Samurai

it can be illustrated by considering the samurai experience with Japanese fencing.

At the low, intermediate, and advanced-intermediate levels of Japanese sword fighting, the outcome is determined by a combination of physical ability (strength, flexibility, and speed) and technique (experience, repertoire, and judgment). In very advanced level contests between evenly matched opponents, other factors come into play. The tolerance for mistakes and windows of opportunity are very small, often only a fraction of an inch or a fraction of a second. These distinctions are practically invisible to the untrained observer. Any mistake like misreading an opponent's intention or miscalculating an attack or defense will probably be fatal since the opponent is unlikely to make an offsetting error.

At this level, the mind itself becomes the battleground. Even pre-conscious thoughts or emotions can alter one's ability to see instantly and respond correctly to events. In this context, not only are gross emotions like terror or rage disastrous, even the briefest fixation of thought is apt to bring ruin. This might involve a partial distraction or fixation on any aspect of oneself or one's opponent. The ability to control one's own mind and to subordinate discriminating thoughts is a necessity for sword combat at a master level. These concepts were articulated by Takuan Soho, the 17th century Zen master in his essays to sword master Yagyu Munenori.

## Introduction

The problem of freeing the mind from emotional and intellectual clutter is similar for both the martial pursuit of advanced swordsmanship and the Zen pursuit of spiritual enlightenment.

Yagyu Munenori captured this concept in a poem he composed for one of his sons.

> Behind the technique, know that there
> is the spirit.
> It is dawning now.
> Open the curtain
> and see, the moonlight is shining in!

This context of mortal combat established the personal case for the affinity between the samurai and Zen. Unlike the samurai's vassal role in the feudal system, the samurai's personal role as a martial artist demonstrates an inherent affinity to Zen that is still applicable today. This legacy can be found in the many thousands of contemporary martial artists who have progressed through their training to advanced levels of their respective arts.

# Zen Stories of the Samurai

**Zen Master Bodai Daruma**

# Teachers and Disciples

*In contemporary society, we sometimes look at learning as a process, teachers as providers, knowledge as a commodity, and the student as a consumer. In the context of these stories, these modern roles are not appropriate. For both Zen and the martial arts, the students are not consumers; rather each student is the subject of a transformation process.*

*Zen Stories of the Samurai*

# Preparing for Training

The famous sword master, Yagyu Munenori, was not pleased with his son Matajuro's progress in fencing. He attributed Matajuro's lack of progress to a lack of effort. As a result, Master Yagyu considered Matajuro to be a family failure.

This embarrassed and angered Matajuro. He was determined to prove his father wrong. Matajuro left his home and journeyed to a distant province where he had heard of a sword master named Master Banzo.

When Matajuro arrived in the province, he stopped at the local temple. The monks told him that Master Banzo lived as a hermit in the nearby mountains. They warned Matajuro that he was only wasting his time. According to the monks, Master Banzo was now a recluse and he was unlikely to accept Matajuro as a student. Matajuro was not deterred. He followed the path indicated by the monks. By the end of the day, he had located Master Banzo.

Master Banzo gave Matajuro a short interview after which Master Banzo concluded, "I agree with your father, Master Yagyu. You do not have the makings of a top swordsman. You will probably never achieve mastery of the art."

"But, what if I train arduously? Then how long will it take me to become a master swordsman?" Matajuro pleaded.

## Teachers and Disciples

"The rest of your life," replied Master Banzo.

"I can't wait that long," protested Matajuro. "I will accept any hardship. I will become your devoted servant. I will devote myself totally to the study of swordsmanship."

"Oh, in that case," replied Master Banzo, "It will take ten years."

"What if I train twice as hard?" tried Matajuro.

"Then it will take thirty years." replied Master Banzo.

"Why do you say that that?" lamented Matajuro. "First you say ten, then you say thirty years. I will do anything to learn, but I do not have that much time. I must accomplish this within my father's lifetime."

"With that attitude, I expect that it will be closer to seventy years," concluded Master Banzo.

Matajuro was distraught. He had already failed in his father's eyes. Now he was getting off to a very bad start with Master Banzo. Matajuro resolved to persevere and do whatever was required to learn from Master Banzo.

## Zen Stories of the Samurai

After much pleading by Matajuro, Master Banzo finally agreed to let him stay. There was one condition. Master Banzo forbade Matajuro to touch a sword or even talk about swordsmanship.

For the next year, Matajuro served Master Banzo by preparing his meals, cleaning his clothing, and chopping firewood. By that time, Matajuro had become frustrated and depressed to the point where he was at the brink of leaving or even ending his life.

Then, one afternoon, while Matajuro was chopping wood, Master Banzo crept up behind him, picked up a stick, and struck Matajuro painfully on the head.

On the next day, Matajuro was preparing the rice for dinner and Master Banzo attacked him again. Day after day, Master Banzo would creep up on Matajuro and attack him. Master Banzo repeated this morning, noon, and night, whenever Matajuro least expected. Soon Matajuro was forced into a constant state of alertness.

After some months of this unusual training, Matajuro's senses started to sharpen. One morning, when Matajuro was stirring some breakfast food over the fire, Master Banzo crept up and prepared to attack Matajuro from behind.

Without fully being aware of Master Banzo's presence or even turning around, Matajuro instinctively raised the pot lid over his head. The pot lid fended off Master Banzo's blow. Master Banzo was most pleased. "Now," said Master Banzo, "we can begin to work on fencing."

# Understanding the Teaching

Yamoaka Tesshu was one of the last of the samurai. In the course of his life, he served in important governmental posts for both the last feudal Shogunate and for the parliamentary monarchy that replaced it. Master Tesshu was an accomplished individual who attained high levels of mastery in Zen, swordsmanship, and painting.

One day, one of Master Tesshu's fencing students approached him and asked, "Master, what is the essential element of our fencing style that sets it apart from all other schools of swordsmanship?" Master Tesshu replied, "I will not tell you that which should be apparent to you. Tomorrow, do not come to the fencing school. Instead, go to the local temple and pray continuously for the answer to your question. Do this every day. Do not return until you have seen the answer to your question."

The next day, the student did exactly what Master Tesshu had specified. He went to the prescribed temple where he prayed and meditated all day. The student repeated this procedure day after day. After a week of intense effort, the student finally returned to the fencing school.

Upon seeing Master Tesshu, the student reported, "I went to the temple every day and prayed intensely all day long. Even so, no inspiration came to me. Then, yesterday as I was leaving the

## Teachers and Disciples

temple, I noticed the inscription above the shrine. It said: *The Gift of Fearlessness*. Was that what you meant?"

"Exactly!" replied Master Tesshu. "That is the secret of our fencing style. However, it is important that you understand this fully. In other fencing schools, some warriors are not afraid to face enemies who are armed with swords. Yet these same warriors are afraid to face their own passions and delusions. In our way of fencing, we are never afraid to face either our external enemies or our own inner enemies."

# Searching for a Successor

A samurai named Tsukahara Bokuden was a master swordsman and founder of his own style of swordsmanship. At one point in his career, Master Bokuden decided to select the person who would eventually succeed him as head of his fencing school.

In those days, it was the custom for the head of a fencing school to pass the leadership to a close family member. Fortunately, Master Bokuden had three sons, all of whom were advanced fencing students. For Master Bokuden, it was a given that his successor should be an expert fencer. More significantly, Master Bokuden wanted a successor who understood the underlying principles of the art and could exemplify them in every day activities.

Master Bokuden decided to test his sons for these qualities by calling each one in for a private interview. The place that Master Bokuden selected was a small room with only one door. On the inside of the room was a curtain that covered the doorway. Before each son arrived, Master Bokuden balanced a small pillow upon the curtain over the doorway. He carefully arranged curtain and pillow so that the slightest movement of the curtain would dislodge the pillow; causing it to fall on the head of any person entering the room.

When everything was ready, Master Bokuden called for his oldest son. As his son approached, he perceived the pillow on the curtain.

## Teachers and Disciples

The oldest son reached up through the doorway and removed the pillow. Then he entered the room and replaced the pillow exactly where he found it.

Later, Master Bokuden then called his second son. The son had just touched the curtain when he saw the pillow begin to fall. Immediately he caught it and placed it back upon entering the room.

Finally, Master Bokuden then called his third son. The third son pushed the curtain open and the pillow hit him on the head. However, his reflexes were so quick that he was able to draw his sword and cut the pillow in half before it reached the floor.

Then Master Bokuden called all of his sons together and spoke to them. "Eldest son, you are well qualified to lead my school." Then Master Bokuden gave him a sword. Next Master Bokuden said, "Second son, you are progressing in your training. Persevere and continue to study hard." Then Master Bokuden severely reprimanded the youngest son for disgracing the family by his poor performance.

# Learning from the Penitent

A samurai named Zenkai was the retainer of a high official in the capital. Zenkai had fallen in love with the official's wife, which was later discovered by the official. To save himself, Zenkai slew the official. Then Zenkai ran away with the official's wife.

This was a high crime in feudal Japan. Their life on the run led them both to become outcasts and thieves. After they settled into a life of crime, the woman became so greedy that over time even Zenkai grew disgusted with her. Zenkai eventually abandoned her. Then he journeyed far away and became a wandering monk.

To atone for his past misdeeds, Zenkai resolved to accomplish some significant good deed in his lifetime. In the course of his wanderings, Zenkai learned about a dangerous road along a cliff. Landslides and washouts along this cliff road had caused the injury and death of many travelers. Zenkai resolved to cut a tunnel through the mountain so that travelers could avoid the cliff road and cross the mountain safely.

Begging for food and construction materials in the daytime, Zenkai worked alone at night digging his tunnel. When thirty years had gone by, the tunnel was twenty feet high, thirty feet wide and 2,280 feet long.

## Teachers and Disciples

Two years before the work was completed, Zenkai was discovered by the son of the man he had murdered. The son confronted Zenkai and proclaimed his right to kill Zenkai in revenge.

"I will give you my life willingly," said Zenkai. "Only let me finish this work. On the day it is completed you may kill me without further delay."

The son agreed to this condition and waited day after day. Several months passed and Zenkai kept on digging. Eventually, the son grew tired of sitting and watching and began to help with the digging. After more than a year of helping on the tunnel project, the son came to admire Zenkai's strong will and reformed character.

Finally, the tunnel was completed and the people could use it to travel in safety.

Zenkai approached the official's son and said, "Now cut off my head. My work is done."

"How can I cut off my own teacher's head?" asked the younger man with tears in his eyes.

# Zen Stories of the Samurai

**Hotei Observing A Butterfly**

# Insights

*Once the mind has been cleared of distractions, it is possible to perceive things as they actually are. The distinction between intuition and cognition begins to disappear. This higher level of perception is essential for martial arts masters and is a characteristic of advanced training in both Zen and in the martial arts.*

# Trusting Intuition

Yagyu Munenori was a high-ranking samurai and a master swordsman. One spring day, Master Yagyu decided to walk out into his garden in order to observe and reflect on the cherry blossoms. As was his custom, Master Yagyu asked his page to come along.

The page was a young samurai boy, whose job it was to perform minor services for his lord. The page carried Master Yagyu's meditation cushion while they walked. Then, while Master Yagyu was sitting in meditation, the page held his master's long sword while standing a short distance behind him.

As Master Yagyu sat down and began to contemplate the cherry blossoms, the page's mind began to wander. Eventually, the page started to daydream and speculate, "Although he is the greatest swordsman in all Japan, my master would certainly be vulnerable to an attack by me while he is unarmed and so entranced by the cherry blossoms."

Suddenly, Master Yagyu's concentration was broken and he began to look around as if he had lost something. Not finding anything amiss and feeling quite restless, Master Yagyu, followed by the page, quietly left the garden, and returned to his other duties.

Over the course of the day, Master Yagyu's retainers noticed that he seemed irritated. They discussed the matter among themselves

## Insights

and decided that the senior retainer should speak to the Master and see what the problem might be.

The senior retainer asked Master Yagyu why he appeared distressed.

Master Yagyu answered, "Oh, everything is going well enough, but I am disturbed because of a feeling that I cannot explain. In my many years as a swordsman, I have acquired the ability to sense my opponents' intentions and anticipate their moves against me. I have learned to trust these instincts completely."

"Then," Master Yagyu continued, "this morning, when I was in the garden, I felt a sudden sense of imminent danger as if I were the target of an impending attack. I searched the area and found that there was no one concealed. Now I am angry with myself because I can not determine the reason for my feelings."

The senior retainer related the story to the other members of the staff and eventually word filtered down and reached the young page. When the page heard the story of Master Yagyu's premonition, the page went to see Master Yagyu. Apologizing profusely, the page confessed to Master Yagyu, telling him about his own thoughts earlier that morning in the garden. Instead of reprimanding the page, Master Yagyu was pleased that his apperception was not off the mark. "Now I understand," he mused out loud.

❖❖❖❖

*Zen Stories of the Samurai*

# Perceiving Mastery

Yagyu Munenori was a great swordsman and held the prestigious position of official fencing instructor to Tokugawa Iyemitsu, the Shogun.

It happened one day that a retainer of the Shogun approached Munenori asking for fencing lessons.

Munenori's mastery of swordsmanship was so advanced that he could determine the quality of a person's fencing ability simply by watching them walk or perform other every day activities.

"As I observe you, you seem to already be a master of swordsmanship yourself," Munenori replied when he heard the retainer's request. "Please tell me what styles of fencing you have studied."

The retainer quietly replied, "I am ashamed to admit that I have never formally studied swordsmanship."

"Is this a poor attempt at false modesty or dare you try to fool me?" challenged Munenori. "I am the personal instructor to the Shogun himself and my judgment in these matters never fails!"

## Insights

"I am sorry to offend your honor, but I really know nothing of fencing," assured the retainer.

The resolute denial on the part of the guard had such a ring of sincerity that it made Munenori think for a while. Finally, Munenori addressed the guard, "If you say so, then it must be the case. However, I still believe that you are a master of something, although I am not yet sure of what."

The guard considered what Munenori had said and offered, "There is one thing that I have dedicated my life to achieving. When I was still a boy, the thought came to me that under no circumstances should a samurai be afraid of death. For years, I have grappled with this problem. Finally, the problem of fearing death has entirely ceased to worry me. Maybe this is what you perceive?"

"Exactly!" exclaimed Munenori. "That is precisely what I mean. I am glad that I made no mistake in my judgment. The ultimate secrets of swordsmanship also lie in releasing all attachments to thoughts of life and death. I have trained ever so many students along this line, but none has advanced to the final certificate of mastery in swordsmanship. You need no technical training. You are already a master!"

# Releasing the Mind

In Japanese archery, the moment that the arrow is released is one in which the mind should have no attachments. Zen Master Bukkoku Kokushi used poetry to teach about archery and life.

> The bow is broken.
>
> Arrows are all gone.
>
> This critical moment:
>
> Possess no fainting heart.
>
> Shoot with no delay.

In another poem, Master Bukkoku said:

> No target is erected.
>
> No bow is drawn.
>
> The arrow leaves the string.
>
> It may not hit,
>
> but it does not miss!

**Insights**

# Discerning Intentions

Lord Taiko was both a warlord and a devoted student of Tea Master Sen no Rikyu.

One of Lord Taiko's retainers was a samurai named Kato. Kato had no understanding of the tea ceremony and he was greatly bothered by Lord Taiko's preoccupation with it.

"My Lord Taiko has many more important matters to be concerned with," thought Kato. "The affairs of our province will certainly be neglected if he continues to waste his time on this trivial pastime. If our enemies hear of his obsession, they will think that he has grown weak and our province will be subject to attack."

Over time, Lord Taiko's dedication to the tea ceremony continued to bother Kato, yet etiquette prevented him from openly confronting or correcting Lord Taiko. Finally, Kato came up with a solution.

"If I were to kill Master Rikyu," reasoned Kato, "then there would be no one to encourage my Lord Taiko in his foolish pursuit of the tea ceremony." With that in mind, Kato made an appointment to visit Master Rikyu with the secret intention of killing him.

## Zen Stories of the Samurai

When Kato arrived at the teahouse, it was already evening. Master Rikyu greeted him outside. "Please, come in," invited Master Rikyu. "I will perform the tea ceremony for you."

In feudal Japan, it was the custom for "off duty" samurai to remove their long swords before going indoors. Special sword racks were kept at the entryways of samurai homes and public places. Interior spaces in early Japanese architecture were generally small. This was particularly true of tea houses. Besides the awkwardness of a long sword in such a confined space, the peaceful nature of a teahouse would make sword wearing most inappropriate.

As Kato prepared to enter the teahouse, Master Rikyu pointed out the sword rack by the door. Kato rebuffed Master Rikyu's guidance. "I am a samurai and I always have my sword with me, tea ceremony or not."

"Very well," consented Master Rikyu. "Bring your sword into the teahouse with you and I will begin serving."

Master Rikyu already had a charcoal fire started and Kato sat in the designated place adjacent to it. As he began the tea preparation Master Rikyu demonstrated the grace and composure for which he was renowned. His movements were effortless and precise.

Suddenly, Master Rikyu's arm knocked against a container of water. The container tipped over, dumping its contents onto the hot charcoal fire. Hissing steam released a charcoal ash cloud that

**Insights**

filled the small teahouse.

In the blinding confusion Kato ran out of the teahouse door. The tea-master was only a few steps behind Kato in leaving the teahouse.

"Oh, I am so sorry," apologized Master Rikyu. "It was my mistake. Please come back inside with me and we will finish having our tea." Pausing a moment, the tea master brought his arm around from behind him. He was holding Kato's sword, still in its scabbard. "Please don't worry about your sword, I have it right here with me. The scabbard and hilt have been covered with ashes. I'll see that it is properly cleaned and returned to you."

Kato realized the futility of his attempt on Master Rikyu's life and his perception of the tea ceremony was forever altered.

**Zen Stories of the Samurai**

**Hotei Laughing**

# Monk Encounters

*The interactions between Zen monks and samurai could be intense and dramatic. Some of the methods employed by these early Japanese Zen masters might seem unusual and even extreme by today's standards.*

**Zen Stories of the Samurai**

# Knowing and Not-Knowing

Master Bankei was the head monk at the Zen monastery at Korinji. Periodically, Master Bankei would leave the monastery and travel around the capital city. There he would teach the public about Zen. In the capital were many samurai from different fencing schools. Many of these samurai were among those who would attend Master Bankei's lessons.

One day a samurai arrived for an audience with Master Bankei. As the samurai approached Master Bankei, the samurai pulled out his folding fan and held it out in front of Master Bankei.

"Master," challenged the samurai, "When this object appears before us, we call it a fan. Yet, before time began, it was non-existent. What was its nature the instant that it was initially constructed?"

Master Bankei replied, "I know."

"What do you know?" asked the samurai.

Master Bankei answered, "I know that I do not know."

**Monk Encounters**

The samurai looked up with admiration and said, "Ah! Confucius himself said that wisdom is the ability to admit that you do not know something."

Shaking his head, Master Bankei contradicted the samurai. "That is not it at all."

**Zen Stories of the Samurai**

# Penetrating Defenses

A samurai who was also a fencing master had an audience with Master Bankei.

"After years of training," began the samurai, "I have reached the stage where my hands respond perfectly according to my mind. Now I am at a level of skill where I can defeat opponents without even picking up my sword. My very gaze pierces them to their bones and disrupts them completely. It is like the same penetrating look that you yourself use to assess the depth of a person's state of enlightenment."

Master Bankei then congratulated the samurai. "You certainly have done very well in your pursuit of the martial arts." He paused for a moment. "Now, attack me!"

The samurai was completely flustered by Master Bankei's sudden challenge. He could not speak a word in response.

Master Bankei said, "I have just delivered my blow."

The samurai immediately recovered his composition, bowed, and responded, "Amazing! Your attack is as swift as lightning, as quick as a spark from a flint. Your mastery is much greater than mine.

## Monk Encounters

I humbly beg you to teach me the essence of Zen."

# Zen Stories of the Samurai

# Sustaining Concentration

Yamana Morofuyu was a samurai in the service of the Ashikaga clan. He had held a command position as a naval commander and later he was reassigned to lead a cavalry unit. Concurrent with that new assignment, Morofuyu took up the study of Zen.

Every year, the local temple held a special weeklong Zen training session commemorating the anniversary of Buddha's enlightenment. On one such occasion, Morofuyu came to the temple, but he would not sit in the meditation hall with the other samurai Zen students. Instead, he stayed mounted on horseback and spent the day practicing his horsemanship by riding around the temple compound and the adjoining grounds.

Zen Master Daikyo was the head of the temple and observed Morofuyu's unorthodox behavior. He warned Morofuyu, saying, "On horseback your concentration will be easily distracted. Perform your meditation by sitting in the meditation hall."

Morofuyu replied, "Monks are men of sitting, and should certainly do their meditation in the meditation hall. I however am a samurai and I should practice meditation on horseback."

"So, samurai!" retorted Master Daikyo. "You were formerly a naval captain, and now you are a cavalry officer. Tell me this: Bodai

## Monk Encounters

Daruma's coming to China from India, over the waves or by horseback, is the meaning the same or different?"

Morofuyu did not know what to say. Thereupon, Master Daikyo snatched up Morofuyu's riding crop from his saddle and hit him with it saying, "Oh, go ride away, go ride away."

# Meaning and Mind

A samurai named Yamamoto Gorozaemon requested an interview with Zen Master Tetsugyu. Gorozaemon asked Master Tetsugyu, "Master, tell me something about Zen?"

Master Tetsugyu replied, "Zen gets rid of the discriminating mind. It is nothing more than that. Here is an example that a samurai might appreciate. The Chinese character for the word *cowardice* is made of the character for *meaning* added to the character for *mind*. For a thing to have meaning, a person must intellectually discriminate between different thoughts. In a similar fashion, when people attach discrimination to their true minds, they become cowardly. Can a samurai follow his path with courage if he accepts discrimination in his true mind? You should be able to develop an idea of Zen from this example."

**Monk Encounters**

# Unblocking the Imagination

Shoju Ronin, the Zen Master, was approached by a samurai who was looking for advice. Introducing himself to Master Ronin, the samurai explained his problem.

"Ever since my youth," began the samurai. "I have been disciplining myself through the study of swordsmanship. For over 20 years, I trained in a number of different fencing schools until I had mastered all of their secrets. I now have a great desire to establish a school of my own and I have been devoting a great amount of work to making this happen."

Master Ronin sat quietly as the samurai continued. "My problem is this. In spite of my best efforts, I have not been able to articulate the true essence of my school. I need to be able to describe that which clearly distinguishes it from all others. Is it possible for you to teach me a way to find the answer?"

After listening very attentively, Master Ronin stood up and walked over to where the samurai was sitting. Next, Master Ronin hit the samurai three times very hard with his fists and then proceeded to kick him so that he toppled over onto the floor.

The rough treatment caused the samurai to have a sudden enlightenment and instantly he had new insight into his fencing art.

**Monk Encounters**

# Moving Freely

Word of Master Ronin's unusual teaching methods spread around the garrison town and sparked the interest of the local samurai. As a result, many of these samurai began to approach Master Ronin for instructions in Zen. One day a group of his samurai Zen students invited Master Ronin to tea. When they had finished their tea, they all went to a courtyard and watched a series of fencing matches.

After several matches, one of the samurai expressed an opinion to Master Ronin.

"You are certainly a great master of Zen and as far as theory is concerned, you are unsurpassed. However, when it comes to the real use of the sword, there would be no way that you could avoid defeat from professionals like us."

Master Ronin replied, "If you wish to strike at me, you may try to do so. However, I do not believe that you will succeed."

The samurai looked at each other cautiously, "Would you really allow us to challenge you?" they asked.

"Yes!" asserted Master Ronin.

## Zen Stories of the Samurai

The samurai rose and prepared for a contest. They offered a sword for Master Ronin to use but he refused, saying, "I follow the way of Buddha and will not take up a weapon."

Reaching into his sash, Master Ronin pulled out a small brush with long flowing horse tail bristles, used to shoo flies.

"Here," said Master Ronin. "Let me substitute my fly chaser for a sword. Don't worry. If you hit me, I will acknowledge your skill and not claim that I was handicapped by improper equipment nor by some other disadvantage."

The samurai took up their swords and each one in succession attempted to strike down Master Ronin. To their great surprise, Master Ronin presented no opening for an attack and his fly chaser seemed everywhere, threatening them wherever they were vulnerable. Finally, after many attempts, the samurai admitted defeat.

After the match, Master Ronin returned to the monastery. Later, one of his fellow monks asked Master Ronin about his experience with the samurai. "In terms of Zen, there is nothing that I can say to doubt your superiority," began the monk, "but how did you manage to hold your own in that fencing contest?"

Master Ronin replied, "When correct insight is gained and is not obstructed by discrimination, it can be applied to anything, including swordsmanship. With clear insight, the nature of the

## Monk Encounters

sword is seen and it movements are at once known. However fast or complex those movements might be, there is no being confused about their timing or destination."

# Zen Stories of the Samurai

# Understanding by Being

A samurai named Nobushige approached Zen Master Hakuin.

"Tell me, Master," began Nobushige. "Is there really a heaven and a hell?"

Master Hakuin replied, "Who are you?"

"I am a samurai!" Nobushige replied.

"You a samurai?" asked Master Hakuin indignantly. "By your bearing I could not imagine that any warlord would have you as a retainer. Your entire appearance is uncouth and unworthy of a samurai; even your face is too ugly. Truly, your calling must be that of a beggar."

Nobushige was outraged at the insult and breach of etiquette and reflexively reached across to his sword and grabbed the hilt.

Raising his voice, Master Hakuin taunted, "Oh! So you have a sword. An inept imposter such as you has probably let it grow rusty and dull through neglect. Truly your weapon is as useless as your fencing skills and not even capable of cutting off my head!"

**Monk Encounters**

Nobushige was enraged at these remarks. His sword now was completely drawn and raised over his head, ready to strike down on Master Hakuin.

At that moment, Master Hakuin calmly added, "Here open the gates of hell."

Upon hearing this, Nobushige realized at once that Master Hakuin's remarks had been a teaching technique. Nobushige immediately sheathed his sword, dropped to his knees, and bowed to Master Hakuin. At that point, Master Hakuin concluded, "Here open the gates of Heaven."

# Zen Stories of the Samurai

**Monk Sleeping on a Tiger**

# Kenchoji Temple

*In 1253, the Chinese Zen missionary Rankei Doryu established the main temple for the Rinzai branch of Zen. Shogun Hojo Tokiyori sponsored the construction. Kenchoji Temple has survived numerous wars, fires, and earthquakes.*

*The Buddhist saint, Jizo, is the patron of the Kenchoji Temple. "Jizo" means "Earth Womb" indicating a pre-Buddhist fertility goddess origin. Japanese Buddhists consider Jizo as protector of and intercessor for the weak, oppressed, or threatened. This includes young children, firefighters, travelers, and people condemned to hell.*

*Kenchoji Temple contains many fine statues of Jizo. In art, Jizo is often depicted as a young boy, wearing a long-sleeved monk's robe. He frequently carries a jewel in one hand and a pilgrim's jingle staff with metal rings on top in the other. The light of the jewel and the sound of the staff symbolize the truth that awakens people from their delusions.*

*Every February, the transition from winter to spring is celebrated at the Setsubun festival. In feudal times, the holiday was an opportunity for self-purification before the spring planting. Celebrants shout, "In with good fortune, out with demons!" At Kenchoji Temple, things are done differently. At Kenchoji, the people only shout "In with good fortune!" Kenchoji Temple's mission of compassion does not deny ministry, even to demons.*

*Zen Stories of the Samurai*

# Going Beyond the Ordinary

In Japan there is an annual memorial holiday called Segaki that commemorates the dead, particularly the forgotten dead. On Segaki, people go to their local temple and perform a ritual where they offer food while reciting prayers. On one particular Segaki, when Zen Master Rankei was in charge of Kenchoji Temple, a samurai rushed in just as Master Rankei had concluded the annual ritual.

"You have missed the ceremony," Master Rankei informed the samurai.

"That is awful," lamented the distressed samurai. "I needed to attend the ceremony by any means."

Master Rankei was very moved by the samurai's sincerity, so he agreed to perform the ceremony all over again, just for the samurai. At the end of the ritual, the samurai humbly thanked Master Rankei.

Just as he was leaving the temple, the samurai turned toward Master Rankei and proclaimed, "I am the ghost of Kagetoki Kajiwara, faithful samurai retainer to the late Shogun Yoritomo Minamoto. Due to your compassion, I have now fulfilled my obligation to my deceased lord."

## Kenchoji Temple

The mysterious samurai disappeared and was never seen again. Ever since that time, Kenchoji Temple has maintained the unusual custom of always performing the Segaki ceremony twice.

## Puzzling Achievement

When Zen Master Ichigen was head of Kenchoji Temple, he tested his students with this Zen puzzle.

"Long ago," began Master Ichigen, "during the time when the warlord Nitta Sadayoshi's armies were attacking the capital, they burned down all of the Buddhist temples in their path. It is claimed that when Lord Sadayoshi's samurai began to set fire to Kenchoji Temple, the monk responsible for the main hall put the statue of Jizo on his back and carried it out of danger."

Master Ichigen continued, "That statue was sixteen feet high and weighed over 800 pounds. The doors to the hall had only an eight-foot opening. How did the monk carry Jizo through the opening?"

**Kenchoji Temple**

# Clearing Confusion

A samurai named Sakawa Koresda, from the Uesugi clan, came to the Kenchoji Temple complex. He entered the main hall, and began to pray at the shrine of Jizo-of-a-Thousand-Forms. After he had finished praying, Sakawa went over to see the Zen monk who was in charge of the main hall. Sakawa then asked the monk this question: "Of the thousand manifestations of Jizo, which one is the supreme?"

Pointing to Sakawa, the attending monk fired back, "Inside this samurai that I see in front of me, there are a thousand thoughts and ten thousand imaginings. Which of these is supreme?"

Sakawa had no answer for the monk.

The attending monk continued, "Of the thousand manifestations of Jizo, the supreme Jizo is the Buddha-nature that is always using those thousand manifestations."

Sakawa then asked, "What is this Buddha-nature?"

In response, the attending monk suddenly reached out and tweaked Sakawa's nose.

Immediately Sakawa had a realization.

**Kenchoji Temple**

# Making Jizo Stand

While Zen Master Yakkoku was head of the Kenchoji Temple, a civil war had broken out in the region around the temple. The devastation that accompanied the conflict brought hard times to the temple.

In addition to the overall problems that were besetting the monastery, Zen Master Yakkoku himself had been very ill. One winter day, Master Yakkoku got out of his sick bed and preached a sermon to the entire assembly at the monastery. In his sermon, he said, "Oh men of great virtue, I ask this of you: Make the seated image of Jizo in this great hall stand up!"

For years afterward, this particular line from Master Yakkoku's sermon became a Zen riddle. It was used at Kenchoji Temple to help clear the minds of Zen practitioners from discriminating thoughts.

Some time after Master Yakkoku's sermon, a samurai, named Mamiya Munekatsu, resolved to make the statue of the seated Jizo stand up. Munekatsu proceeded to confine himself to the great hall of Kenchoji Temple for twenty-one days of fasting and prayer. Munekatsu continuously chanted a mantra by repeating the name of Great Vow, which is an alias for Jizo. Legend holds that Jizo acquired this alias because he refused to enter Buddhist heaven until all of the residents of all hells had been saved. By the end of the twenty-one days, Munekatsu's chanting had grown wild and he ran up and down the great hall like a lunatic, shouting, "Holy Jizo! Stand up!"

At two o'clock in the morning, an attending monk made the rounds and as per temple custom, he signaled the hour by sounding the wooden clapper in the front of the great hall. "Clack!" At that sound, Munekatsu had an immediate insight and exclaimed aloud, "Holy Jizo! It is not that Jizo stands up. It is not that Jizo sits down. He has a life that is neither standing nor sitting."

**Kenchoji Temple**

# Underestimating Loyalty

When Zen Master Toden was head of Kenchoji Temple, a swaggering samurai named Yoriyasu requested an audience with him.

At that audience, Yoriyasu asked Master Toden to explain Zen. Master Toden admonished him by saying, "The word *loyalty* is composed of the characters for *center* and *heart*. The implications of this are that the warlord's interests are at the center of every samurai. When I observe samurai today, I see that many of their hearts crave money, sex, and alcohol. With others, their hearts lust for fame, power, and status. By allowing their passions to pull at their hearts from all directions, these samurai have lost the ability to center their hearts. As a result, these samurai will not manifest true loyalty. If you, Yoriyasu, sincerely wish to practice Zen, then first practice loyalty and do not slip into wrong desires."

Yoriyasu was annoyed at having his inquiry answered by such a lecture. "A samurai's loyalty is demonstrated by his actions on the battlefield. What need has a samurai for a sermon from a priest?" retorted Yoriyasu.

Master Toden replied dismissively, "You, Sir are a samurai in turmoil. I am a gentleman of peace. We can have nothing of interest to say to each other."

Yoriyasu then drew his sword and held it out saying, "A samurai's loyalty is in his sword. If you do not understand even this, then you have no business talking about loyalty at all."

Referring to an old Chinese story about a magical sword that could banish demons, Master Toden responded, "This old priest has the treasure sword of the Diamond King. If you do not know what that is, then it is you that have no standing upon which to talk about the meaning of loyalty."

"Loyalty of your Diamond Sword!" Yoriyasu scoffed. "Of what use are such folk tales in actual fighting?"

At that point, Master Toden suddenly jumped forward and gave a mighty shout. The sound penetrated Yoriyasu with such force that he was knocked down and lost consciousness.

After a little while, Master Toden gave another shout and Yoriyasu regained consciousness. When he came to, Master Toden asked him, "That loyalty, which is in the samurai's sword, where is it right now? Answer!"

Yoriyasu had no reply. He was awestruck. He apologized to Master Toden and quickly left.

**Kenchoji Temple**

# Persevering to the End

Tadamasa was a senior retainer to the powerful warlord Hojo Takatoki. In addition to being a samurai, Tadamasa was an advanced practitioner of Zen and often meditated at Kenchoji Temple.

When a civil war broke out in the area around Kenchoji Temple, Tadamasa took part in the fighting and became wounded during a battle.

Immediately after the battle, and still dressed in his armor, the injured Tadamasa galloped back to Kenchoji Temple to see Zen Master Sozan.

Master Sozan was in the middle of a tea ceremony as Tadamasa came through the door. Master Sozan immediately placed a teacup in front of Tadamasa and asked him, "How does it stand with you?"

Tadamasa stamped on the teacup, smashed it, and said "Heaven and earth are altogether broken up!"

Master Sozan again asked, "When heaven and earth are broken up, how does it stand with you?"

Tadamasa responded by crossing his hands over his chest while standing in front of Master Sozan. Master Sozan reached out and hit him, causing Tadamasa to wince from the pain of his wounds.

"Heaven and earth are not quite broken up yet," added Master Sozan.

Just at that point, a signal drum sounded from the military camp and Tadamasa rushed off to rejoin his unit for the next battle.

The following evening, Tadamasa again returned to see Master Sozan at Kenchoji Temple. Tadamasa had been wounded again and was now disheveled and covered with blood.

As soon as Master Sozan saw Tadamasa, he once more asked, "When heaven and earth are broken up, how does it stand with you?"

Tadamasa propped himself up in front of Master Sozan by leaning on his sword. Then Tadamasa gave a great shout and died.

# High and Mighty

**Moon, Reflection, and Monkey Artist**

# High and Mighty

*The spread of Zen in feudal Japan was encouraged by the highest levels of the Shogun's military government. As is often the case, associating a religious system too closely with the ruling powers raises issues for both the religion and the political power elite.*

*In these stories, the demands of secular power confront Zen practitioners.*

**High and Mighty**

# Cutting Off Fear

Zen Master Bukko Kokushi was one of the Chinese missionaries who introduced Zen to Japan. One of Master Bukko's students was Hojo Tokimune, who was filling the role of Shogun. It was during Lord Tokimune's administration that Japan faced one of its greatest national crises - the Mongol invasions.

On one occasion, Lord Tokimune asked Master Bukko, "Master, fear is the worst enemy of my life. How can I free myself from it?"

Master Bukko replied, "Cut it off at its source."

Then Lord Tokimune asked, "Where does it come from?"

"It comes from Tokimune himself," replied Master Bukko.

"Above all things, I hate fear the most," declared Shogun Tokimune. "How can I possibly be the source of it?"

Master Bukko replied, "See how you feel when you abandon this precious self which you know as Tokimune. Go off and do that; see me again when you have finished."

"How can I possibly accomplish this?" asked the Shogun.

# Zen Stories of the Samurai

Master Bukko replied, "Shut out all of your thoughts."

Lord Tokimune asked, "How do I turn off my thinking?"

Master Bukko replied, "Sit cross-legged in meditation and look into the source of all of the thoughts that you imagine as belonging to Tokimune."

Shogun Tokimune lamented, "My official duties leave me with so little time that is difficult to spare even a moment for meditation."

Master Bukko advised, "Whatever worldly affairs you engage in, make them an instrument of meditation. Use them as opportunities for inner reflection and some day you will find out who this beloved Tokimune really is."

Time passed and Lord Tokimune continued his Zen studies. Eventually, Japanese military intelligence received word that the Mongol invasion force had departed from Korea and was headed for Japan. Lord Tokimune again called on Master Bukko for an audience. This time, the Lord Tokimune arrived in full armor and ready for war.

"Master, the most important event of my life has arrived!" announced Lord Tokimune.

## High and Mighty

Master Bukko inquired, "How will you face it?"

Lord Tokimune focused all of his energy, stamped his feet, and gave a tremendous shout. It was as if the shout scared away an invisible enemy in front of him.

"Truly, a lion's cub roars like a lion. Dash straight forward and do not look back!" exhorted Master Bukko.

# Reevaluating the Beautiful

The warlord Toyotomi Hideyoshi assumed control of Japan after the death of Shogun Nobunaga. Although a warrior with a lower class background, Hideyoshi was a student of Zen and had an appreciation for the arts. His interests in this area included both the tea ceremony and flowers.

Lord Hideyoshi had a long-standing relationship with the founder of the tea ceremony, Master Sen no Rikyu. Not only was he an expert in the tea ceremony, Tea Master Rikyu was an exceptional gardener. One year, Lord Hideyoshi received word that Master Rikyu's garden contained a large and spectacular display of morning glories. Lord Hideyoshi sent word to Master Rikyu that he would like to come and view the morning glories.

Master Rikyu would not respond to the request and did not invite Lord Hideyoshi to view the garden. Lord Hideyoshi sent more messages, and Master Rikyu ignored them all. Finally, Lord Hideyoshi became impatient. Not only was Master Rikyu being uncooperative to the supreme ruler of the nation, but also the season of the morning glories' peak beauty would soon be past. Lord Hideyoshi sent word to Master Rikyu that he was coming to view the morning glories, invitation or not.

The next morning, Lord Hideyoshi arrived at the teahouse where Master Rikyu greeted him. Master Rikyu led Lord Hideyoshi to the

## High and Mighty

garden behind the teahouse. When they entered, all that Lord Hideyoshi saw was one morning glory and a simple place to sit. Just prior to Lord Hideyoshi's arrival, Master Rikyu had cut down and removed all of the morning glories except for that one.

"What is the meaning of this!" demanded Lord Hideyoshi.

"My Lord," replied Master Rikyu, "How can we appreciate the beauty of a thousand flowers, if we can not appreciate the beauty of just one?"

Lord Hideyoshi understood at once.

To this day, a Japanese teahouse typically contains a floral arrangement consisting of a single flower.

# Testing for Worthiness

When Lord Masamune ruled over the entire northeastern provinces of Japan, he constructed a temple to commemorate the resting place of his ancestors. Masamune was a student of Zen and wanted to appoint a worthy Zen master to be the abbot of his new family temple.

A monk named Rinan was recommended to Lord Masamune for the position. At the time, Master Rinan was residing in an insignificant temple in a small rural village. Lord Masamune was uncertain of Master Rinan's worthiness for such a prestigious position.

In order to assuage his suspicions, Lord Masamune decided to invite Master Rinan to his castle and surprise him with a test.

When Master Rinan arrived in the provincial capital, an attendant escorted him into the castle. After he arrived at the castle, Master Rinan was then brought into Lord Masamune's audience room.

The audience room was empty and Master Rinan was then directed to proceed into one of the adjoining waiting rooms. The waiting room was also empty, but had an open door leading to yet another room.

## High and Mighty

As Master Rinan entered the doorway, Lord Masamune unexpectedly appeared with a sword drawn overhead. Stepping forward to strike at Master Rinan, Lord Masamune shouted, "What would you say at this moment of life and death?"

Master Rinan, seemingly unmoved by this unusual and dangerous greeting, instantly stepped in under the path of the sword, reached his arm around Lord Masamune's waist, and gave Lord Masamune a severe shaking.

The great warlord exclaimed, "What a dangerous trick you play!"

Master Rinan abruptly pushed Lord Masamune away, retorting, "Oh, this pretentious man!"

# Zen Stories of the Samurai

## Commanding the Elusive

The warlord Riko was a samurai and a student of Zen. He became aware of the arrival of a famous Zen Master named Yakusan to a mountain monastery in a remote part of his province.

Lord Riko wanted to meet Master Yakusan and sent several invitations the Zen master, asking him to come to the provincial capital. Master Yakusan, however, did not respond to these invitations. Lord Riko was offended and grew impatient.

Finally, Lord Riko determined that he would confront the monk, and he headed for the mountain monastery with the intention of demanding an audience.

When Lord Riko arrived at the monastery, he was greeted unceremoniously by novice monks who asked him to wait. When notified of Lord Riko's arrival, Master Yakusan took no notice and continued to read Buddhist scriptures in his library.

Eventually, an attendant monk brought Lord Riko into the library where Master Yakusan was reading. The attendant then went over to Master Yakusan to remind him that Lord Riko was waiting. Still Master Yakusan kept on with his scripture reading and paid no attention to the presence of the warlord.

## High and Mighty

Lord Riko felt dejected and then became very angry. He indignantly snapped, "Seeing the face is not at all like hearing the name." In effect, Lord Riko was telling Master Yakusan that he was far less impressive in person than his reputation would have led one to believe.

Then Master Yakusan called out, "Oh, Governor!"

Lord Riko answered at once, "Yes, Master?"

Master Yakusan inquired, "Why do you evaluate the hearing over the seeing?"

Lord Riko perceived the lesson in the master's question and apologized.

Lord Riko then asked, "Master, what is the Way?"

Master Yakusan pointed his hand up, and then pointed his hand down. "Do you understand?" the master asked.

"No, Master," replied Lord Riko.

Hearing that, Master Yakusan asserted, "The clouds are in the sky and the water is in the jar."

The interview concluded and Lord Riko returned to the capital satisfied.

**High and Mighty**

# Reprimanding Arrogance

Once a noted Zen master named Yekiwo was traveling through the province controlled by the warlord Uesugi Kenshin. Master Yekiwo had planned to stop in that provincial capital to give a public sermon on the concept of *I know not*. This was a Zen teaching that had been refined many years earlier by Bodai Daruma, one of the founders of Zen.

Lord Uesugi was an adherent of Zen and considered himself an advanced practitioner. Lord Uesugi had heard of Master Yekiwo's reputation and when he became aware of the public sermon, he decided to use the event as an opportunity to test the monk.

When the day came for the sermon, Lord Uesugi disguised himself as a low-ranking samurai. Then he concealed himself among the audience, and listened for a chance to stump Master Yekiwo.

At the conclusion of his sermon, Master Yekiwo followed his normal practice and began to accept questions from the audience. Lord Uesugi saw this as his opportunity to challenge Master Yekiwo. Just as Lord Uesugi was about to ask his question, Master Yekiwo suddenly preempted him.

Turning toward Lord Uesugi, Master Yekiwo demanded, "Oh Lord General! What is the meaning of *I know not?*"

Lord Uesugi was completely taken by surprise and did not know what to say. Thereupon Master Yekiwo continued, "Oh Lord General! Why not give me an answer today, when you talk so glibly about Zen on all other occasions?"

Kenshin resumed his Zen studies in full earnest from that day forward.

## Acting Nobly

In sixteenth century Japan, Takeda Shingen and Uesugi Kenshin were rival warlords in adjoining provinces. Both warlords were ardent practitioners of Zen. While their armies fought on several occasions, the results of their encounters were seldom conclusive since their forces were so evenly matched.

While both lords had shown themselves to be capable of ruthless acts of violence, there were episodes of chivalry between these two mortal enemies.

On one occasion, Lord Takeda found himself fighting two wars at the same time. One was to the north with Lord Uesugi and the other with a coalition of costal provinces to the south. People in Lord Takeda's land-locked province began to suffer greatly from a salt embargo put in place by the southern enemy.

In the north, Lord Uesugi received intelligence about the effect of the embargo. He was outraged, as he preferred to wage his wars on the battlefield and he thought that Lord Takeda's other enemies should do so as well. Lord Uesugi offered to supply Lord Takeda's province with salt; Lord Takeda readily accepted the offer of his rival.

# Seizing the Moment

At another time, Lord Takeda's and Lord Uesugi's armies faced each other in a place called Kawanakajima, between the Sai and Chikuma rivers. This was the fourth time that the two armies had fought at this strategic location.

During the course of this battle, Lord Takeda split the main body of his troops and deployed them well in advance of his command post.

Seizing on this temporary vulnerability, Lord Uesugi himself took lead of a small troop of his personal cavalry and charged through the Takeda lines. Lord Uesugi and his troops breached the defenses and entered Lord Takeda's encampment.

Seeing Lord Takeda sitting on a camp chair, Lord Uesugi galloped past Lord Takeda's personal bodyguards. Not content with the simple imminent prospect of killing his arch adversary and winning the war, Lord Uesugi issued a well-known Zen challenge used to test a student's spontaneity and self-awareness.

Swinging his sword squarely at Lord Takeda's head, he shouted, "What would you say at this moment?"

## High and Mighty

Tradition holds that without rising from his chair, Lord Takeda parried Lord Uesugi's sword by lifting his iron-ribbed war fan while responding, "A snowflake on a blazing stove!"

By that time, reinforcements from the main Takeda force had arrived and Lord Uesugi and his raiding party were forced to withdraw back to their own lines.

# Approaching the Formidable

The Korean ambassador to Japan had presented a number of state gifts to the Japanese Shogun, Tokugawa Iyemitsu. One of these gifts was a large wild tiger. The Shogun and his court were all very impressed by this exotic animal and were awestruck by its graceful beauty, agile strength, and wild ferocity.

One day the Shogun was viewing the tiger in its garden enclosure. Among the Shogun's entourage that day were master swordsman Yagyu Munenori and Zen master Takuan Soho.

The group admired the tiger for a while. Then the Shogun turned to Lord Yagyu. "You have often told me," began the Shogun, "that one of the fundamental principals of your school of fencing maintains that by overcoming attachment to life and death, it is also possible to overcome your adversary without even drawing your sword."

"Yes, my Lord," replied the fencing master. "That is the teaching of my school."

"Then it would please me to see a demonstration," the Shogun ordered. "Proceed into the pen and defeat the tiger without the use of your sword."

## High and Mighty

Lord Yagyu had no choice but to comply, both by virtue of his reputation as a master swordsman and because of his feudal obligations to the Shogun.

As Lord Yagyu cautiously approached the enclosure, the tiger anxiously paced back and forth. An attendant opened the door to the pen and Lord Yagyu walked in smoothly and purposefully. Lord Yagyu's intrusion agitated the tiger, but Lord Yagyu's balanced approach gave the tiger no opening to strike him from either the left or the right. Attuned to the tiger's every movement, Lord Yagyu continued his advance, backing the tiger further into its cage. Finally, the tiger held its ground and was fully coiled and ready to swipe Lord Yagyu. Then with expert timing and without hesitation Lord Yagyu pulled out his folding fan and struck the tiger squarely between the eyes. Stunned and confused, the animal backed off and cowered in the corner of his pen. Taking advantage of his initial success, Lord Yagyu carefully backed out of the pen and returned to where the Shogun and his party were watching in awe.

"Astounding demonstration!" commended the Shogun. "To see that the trained mind could overcome something as formidable as this wild beast is most impressive." Turning his gaze toward the Zen master, the Shogun asked, "Wouldn't you agree, Master Takuan?"

Master Takuan nonchalantly replied, "It was all right."

# Zen Stories of the Samurai

"All right!" exclaimed the Shogun. "Most people would have been killed immediately just by entering the tiger's pen. Perhaps the famous monk thinks he is more capable in this situation than Japan's leading sword master? Certainly you will do me the pleasure of letting me watch you enter the pen and encounter the tiger!" challenged the Shogun.

Master Takuan had well understood the significance of Lord Yagyu's demonstration. In addition to his own personal accomplishments as a Zen master, Master Takuan had been a spiritual advisor to many leading sword masters including Lord Yagyu. Although he was not himself a martial artist, Master Takuan had a keen appreciation for the state of mind associated with advanced levels of swordsmanship and the relationship of that state of mind to the teachings of Zen.

Master Takuan turned to the Shogun, "The fundamental principal of non-attachment to life and death is consistent across both Zen and swordsmanship. However, in Zen, we are not interested in designating adversaries and overcoming them. Rather, we are called with a spirit of compassion to awaken the Buddha nature of all beings."

With that, Master Takuan spit into his hands, rubbed them together, and strolled down to the pen where the attendant let him in the gate. The tiger watched expectantly as Master Takuan serenely entered the pen. Unlike Lord Yagyu's gaze, which was sharp and penetrating, Master Takuan's gaze was relaxed, yet it

# High and Mighty

seemed to fill the whole pen. Master Takuan appeared completely absorbed like a person enjoying the scent of an exquisite blossom.

As the tiger approached Master Takuan, the monk reached out his hand for the tiger to smell. The tiger sniffed Master Takuan's hand, and then licked it. Master Takuan responded by scratching the tiger behind the ears until it started rolling on the ground and purring like a kitten.

Both the Shogun and Lord Yagyu were left in amazement.

**Zen Stories of the Samurai**

# Dispelling Illusions

Tokugawa Iyemitsu, the Japanese Shogun, had a pet monkey. The monkey was very quick. It would dash around the court creating all kinds of mischief. One day the Shogun Iyemitsu issued a challenge for his samurai retainers. "You retainers are the leading samurai of the land," he proclaimed. "See if any of you can match your speed against my monkey."

All of the samurai tried their best, first trying to catch the monkey and then just trying to hit it with a stick. The monkey was too fast, running around the Shogun's court, alternately hiding behind the Shogun's chair and darting out again.

Even the great master swordsman, Yagyu Munenori, joined the chase, but was not able to touch the Shogun's monkey.

By chance, Takuan Soho, the Zen Master, also happened to be at the Shogun's court that day. Finally, after he had become disenchanted with the samurais' lack of skill, Shogun Iyemitsu extended his challenge to Zen Master Takuan. Master Takuan approached the monkey and brandished his monk's staff. Instead of running, the monkey immediately cowered submissively before him.

## High and Mighty

Shogun Iyemitsu was astonished. "How is it that a Zen monk could accomplish what Japan's leading samurai could not?" asked the Shogun.

"That is simple," replied Master Takuan. "All of the samurai were afraid of accidentally hitting you when they chased after the monkey. The monkey was able to perceive this and use it to his advantage. However, when I approached the monkey, he realized that I did not care at all if I struck you."

# Inventing Success

Shogun Tokugawa Iyemitsu liked to host fencing matches at his court. As Shogun, he had access to the best swordsmen in Japan and could arrange some very fine contests.

At one of these events, the Shogun happened to notice the presence of a samurai named Suwa Bunkuro, who was renowned for being a master equestrian. The Shogun asked Bunkuro if he would be taking part in the competition. Bunkuro replied that he would be pleased to participate if he could fight on horseback. Under that condition, assured Bunkuro, he would be able to defeat any of the assembled samurai.

The Shogun was intrigued by the idea and he ordered it to be so. Sure enough, Bunkuro was correct. He was successful in all of his contests. The Shogun's other samurai, while great swordsmen, were not accustomed to fighting while in the saddle and lost their advantage to Bunkuro.

After several matches, the Shogun became irritated by the poor showing of his favorite martial artists. In frustration, the Shogun turned to Yagyu Munenori who was sitting beside him. Lord Yagyu was a fencing master and the Shogun's personal fencing teacher. Although Lord Yagyu did not usually participate in these contests, the Shogun asked him to test his skill against Bunkuro.

## High and Mighty

Lord Yagyu at once agreed and mounted a horse. As Lord Yagyu's horse trotted up to Bunkuro's horse, Lord Yagyu suddenly stopped his horse and slapped Bunkuro's horse's nose with the side of his wooden sword. Bunkuro's horse reared up. As Bunkuro struggled to control his horse, Lord Yagyu knocked Bunkuro off his horse.

# Zen Stories of the Samurai

**Demon Meditating**

# Riff Raff

*Not all samurai fit the stoic, heroic archetype. Cruelty, arrogance, and pride were some of the tendencies that tempted these warriors. These stories tell of some encounters between these less than ideal samurai and Zen practitioners.*

# Exposing the Bully

The samurai Tsukahara Bokuden was a master swordsman. In the course of his career, he crossed swords with as many as two hundred samurai, defeating them all. He also founded his own school of fencing.

On one occasion, Master Bokuden was traveling by boat across Lake Biwa along with a few other passengers. One of the passengers was a particularly crude and belligerent samurai who was boasting about his great fencing skills to anyone who would listen. The farmer and merchant passengers were in fact listening eagerly to the arrogant but exciting stories that the samurai concocted.

Naturally, Master Bokuden was completely disinterested in such bravado. He positioned himself at the other side of the boat and made the most use of his travel time by taking a nap. After a bit, the braggart samurai became bored with awing his civilian audience and noticed Master Bokuden's complete disregard for his antics.

This lack of attention angered the samurai and he walked over to Master Bokuden. Shaking Master Bokuden's shoulder the samurai rudely asked, "You also carry the two swords of the samurai, how is it that you are so disinterested in fencing that you choose not to enter into the conversation?"

# Riff Raff

Master Bokuden responded quietly and politely, "My art is quite different from yours. It consists of not defeating others and not being defeated by others."

The samurai was provoked by this answer and shot back, "What is the name of your fencing school?"

Master Bokuden replied, "Mine is known as the *No Hands School*. This means we defeat the enemy without resorting to our sword."

"Why then do you carry a sword?" asked the samurai.

"This sword," answered Master Bokuden, "is not for defeating others. It is for doing away with my own selfish motives."

By now, the samurai was livid. "So! You expect to fight me without using your sword?"

"Why not?" responded Master Bokuden.

The samurai immediately called to the boatman to steer toward the nearest island where this matter could be settled at once. Master Bokuden cautioned against this, suggesting instead a more remote island where there would be less possibility of any bystanders being hurt.

The boatman complied and steered the boat toward the more remote island. As the boat entered the shallow water around the island, the samurai, eager for combat, jumped out of the boat, drew his sword, and waded to the beach.

Back in the boat, Master Bokuden calmly removed his swords. He handed them to the boatman as he was preparing to disembark.

Suddenly, Master Bokuden grabbed the boatman's oar and pushed it against a rock, sending the boat off into deep water. As the boat glided away from the island and the now stranded samurai, Master Bokuden explained, "This is my *No Hands School*."

**Riff Raff**

# Acting Spontaneously

Zen Master Bankei had a servant who had worked for with him for a many years. While the servant had never taken priestly vows nor become a monk, over time he had become very familiar with the ways of the monks at the Zen temple. One day Master Bankei needed some business taken care of in the city and he dispatched this servant to run the errand.

As the servant prepared for his trip, the temple monks cautioned him to defer his travel until the next morning. By waiting until morning, the monks explained, the servant could avoid traveling through dangerous parts of the city during the night.

During that period in Japan, there were unscrupulous samurai who would practice something called *street-corner killing*. The laws of that time allowed samurai to kill any merchant, farmer, or servant who had shown disrespect toward them. The definition of disrespect was solely at the discretion of the samurai. Some samurai used this prerogative with impunity when they wanted to test the sharpness of a new sword. They would waylay an unsuspecting pedestrian. Then they would try to kill their victim by cutting through them with a single sword stroke. This was known as *street-corner killing*.

Insisting that he would be fine, the servant ignored the monks' advice and started toward the city. By the time the servant

## Zen Stories of the Samurai

reached the city, the sun had already set and it was dark. As the servant moved down the dark street, he felt a hard push and heard a voice hiss, "You have touched me with your sleeve. I will avenge this insult. I will not let you pass." The servant looked and saw a renegade samurai standing there with his sword already drawn and ready to strike.

"But my sleeve did not touch you!" the servant hastily protested.

Then suddenly, without any thought and as if by compulsion, the servant dropped down to his knees and bowed three times to the samurai.

The samurai was overcome with a mixture of surprise and confusion. He sheathed his sword and said, "You are a strange fellow. I will let you go. Leave, get away from here!"

Meanwhile, a merchant staying at a nearby inn had been secretly watching all of this activity. The merchant was seized with a mixture of fear and excitement as he alternately peeked through the window of his room and then hid behind the shutter.

Leaving the samurai behind, the servant rounded the corner and passed by the inn. The awestruck merchant ran out and addressed the servant saying, "I thought you were a dead man for sure. How did you make your escape?"

## Riff Raff

"I live in a temple," replied the servant. "The people there are always making three bows. When I realized that there was nothing I could say to save my life, I just fell into that practice automatically, without any thinking. That is when that samurai called me a strange fellow and let me leave."

# Zen Stories of the Samurai

# Transferring Mastery

Lord Yama no Uchi of Tosa was making his annual trip to the capital to visit the Shogun. On this particular trip, the lord decided to have his tea master accompany him. This way Lord Yama no Uchi could not only enjoy the tea ceremony during his visit, but he would also be able to show off the tea master's skill to the other high-ranking officials while he visited the capital.

The tea master was quite apprehensive about the trip. The capital city was crowded, noisy, and busy, not at all like his quiet country home. The thought of going to a place where he might encounter many samurai from other provinces was very intimidating to the tea master. While he had the favor of his own lord and the respect of his lord's samurai, the tea master himself was not of the samurai class. Should he encounter samurai from other provinces, he would be without protection should they decide to bully him. In fact, the law allowed even the lowest ranking samurai to kill him on the spot if the samurai could claim provocation. The tea master had protested to his lord against going. However, the lord insisted on the tea master's company and the tea master made the trip.

Upon arriving at the capital, the tea master initially spent all of his time in the compound that housed his lord and his retainers. Eventually, Lord Yama no Uchi gave the tea master permission to go out for a day and see some of the city. Although against regulations, the lord gave the tea master permission to dress as a samurai so that he could move more freely around the city.

113

## Riff Raff

As the tea master walked through one of the parks, he felt himself watched by an unemployed samurai with an evil gaze. The tea master tried to avoid the samurai by going another way. However, the samurai homed in on the tea master and forced a conversation. "I see by the emblem on your jacket that you are from Tosa province," said the samurai. "I would be honored if you would accept my challenge to a fencing contest."

The tea master explained his situation. "Although dressed as a samurai, I am really a just a tea master and I have no knowledge of or experience with fencing. So you see I really could not fight with you in a duel."

This news did not deter the unemployed samurai. In fact, he pressed his case even harder. Thinking that he might be able to extort the tea master into buying his way out of the predicament, the samurai became insistent on a duel.

Being completely without options, the tea master relented. "Fine," he said "but first, I have to complete some tasks related to my master's business. You must allow me that time. I will meet you in this park this evening at sunset." The tea master did not want to disgrace either himself or his lord. He therefore resolved to try to die as honorable a death as possible at the hands of this cruel bully.

## Zen Stories of the Samurai

At that point, the tea master had an idea. He remembered a fencing school that he had passed on his way to the park. Perhaps, thought the tea master, the sword master could teach him some rudimentary sword etiquette or some opening movements so that his inevitable death would at least be more dignified. The tea master approached the fencing school and urgently asked one of the students to call for the sword master. When the sword master arrived, he listened quietly while the tea master explained the whole story.

"This is most unusual," mused the sword master. "Most of my students come to me because they want to learn how to use the sword as the means of surviving a conflict. You, however, have come here asking to learn how to die. I will grant your request, but before I do, would you do me the favor of serving me tea?"

The tea master agreed. It was an appropriate exchange of favors between two masters. As the tea master began his preparations, all thoughts of his problems disappeared. He became completely absorbed in the act of the tea ceremony. The sword master watched him closely, observing his serenity and concentration.

Suddenly the sword master slapped his knee and exclaimed, "That is it! You have no need for any further instructions. To die properly you have only to bring to the duel the exact state of mind that you have now. When you meet your opponent, consider him just as you would consider a guest in your teahouse. First, greet him courteously as if you are about to share something very special with him. Then, before the fighting starts, you will make your preparations by taking off your coat, tying back your sleeves, positioning your sword in your belt, and the like. Complete all of these preliminary tasks with the same purposefulness that you would apply to the preparation of tea. Finally, when the time comes and you do draw your sword, simply hold it over your head so that you are ready to strike and wait for your opponent's attack. Make no defense at all. Accept your opponent's attack while you simultaneously strike down on him with all of your concentration. If you are lucky, the duel will end in a mutual kill and you will die with honor."

The tea master thanked the sword master and walked back to the place where he had promised to meet the rogue samurai. When the samurai arrived, the tea master followed the sword master's advice to the letter. The tea master's serene composure greatly disturbed the samurai. The samurai could not understand the tea master's lack of intimidation or the well-paced manner in which the tea master fixed his clothing in preparation for the duel.

Unnerved, the samurai thought, "Surely this is not the same man whom I challenged earlier!"

As they both raised their swords, the samurai saw that he had no opening to attack and that the tea master was completely without fear. Instead of attacking, the samurai backed up and shouted, "I give up!" He then dropped to his knees, bowed, and hastily apologized for his rudeness before hurrying away.

# Zen Stories of the Samurai

**Monk Ripping Scriptures**

# Imminent Death

*With only a moment or two of life remaining, one's thoughts, words, and actions take on additional significance, both for oneself and for those around them.*

# Viewing the World

When the warlord Ouchi Yoshitaka was defeated in battle, he composed this poem just prior to committing suicide. The middle two lines are from the Diamond Sutra, an important Buddhist scripture for many Zen practitioners.

> Both the victor and the vanquished are
>
> but drops of dew,
>
> but bolts of lightning.
>
> So should we view the world.

**Imminent Death**

# Accepting Reality

A minor servant was conducting official business in a neighboring province when he happened to offend a local dignitary. The dignitary was both influential and vindictive. He demanded punishment of the servant.

Under the laws of that time, the warlord of the civil servant's home province was obligated to extradite the servant to the jurisdiction of the dignitary's province.

When the servant reached his home province, his local warlord had already received word of the incident. "It is a pity that I have no authority to help you," said the warlord to his servant. "I am compelled by law to extradite you to that province. Once there, you will face trial and almost certainly be executed."

The warlord continued, "I do have one suggestion. As long as you are going to die anyway, take up a sword and fight me in a duel. If you kill me, then you can surrender yourself to the officials and die with honor."

"What?" exclaimed the servant. "I am not even a samurai and you are an accomplished swordsman! I have never even handled a sword! How could I ever expect to defeat you?"

# Zen Stories of the Samurai

The warlord was in fact a prominent swordsman. He had distinguished himself over the year in many duels. However, he had never encountered one particular situation. He had never faced an opponent who was destined to die no matter what the outcome of the duel. Such an adversary, surmised the warlord, would have no attachment to life and death. As a result, his movements would be totally uninhibited and a worthy test of the warlord's skills.

"Try your luck," replied the warlord. "You certainly have nothing to lose. In any case, you are still in my service and this is what I wish."

So saying, the warlord and the servant retired into the courtyard and took up swords. As they faced off the warlord found himself in an awkward situation. No matter what stance the warlord took, he found himself in a disadvantaged position and was forced to move out of range by stepping backward. Several times the warlord altered his stance and attempted to advance. Each time he found himself in an exposed position and was forced back. Finally, the warlord was cornered at the end of the courtyard and could retreat no further.

This was no longer an amusing exercise in power or an academic test of fencing theory. The warlord was himself facing death and had no option of retreat or rescue. Grasping the true nature of this situation, the warlord shouted a cry of "Ei!" and instantly cut down the servant; killing him with one decisive sword strike.

## Imminent Death

Later on, the warlord reviewed the duel with his military staff. They were all samurai warriors and had a keen interest in fencing. Addressing his military staff, the warlord confessed, "What a desperate situation. I was almost beaten by a civilian, an amateur swordsman! That servant continually moved to positions of advantage with total freedom. May you never find yourselves in a situation like the one that I was facing."

One of the warlord's military aids asked, "When you repeatedly stepped back, was that a ploy on your part, or were you really being driven back by the servant?"

"Truly I was forced back. The servant had placed himself in such commanding positions that I could not have successfully countered his attack and retreat was my only option," replied the warlord.

Another of the warlord's samurai asked, "When you finally shouted 'Ei!' and struck down the servant, had you seen a gap in the servant's defenses?"

"There was no gap or weakness in his position at all," replied the warlord. "I just accepted the reality of the situation without judgment or second thought, allowed my attack to arise spontaneously, and my sword manifested its nature."

# Living with Death

The samurai Ota Dokan was a noted military tactician. He met his end when an enemy stabbed him while he was in a public bath. While grasping the still protruding knife, Dokan recited this poem then died.

> Had I known
>
> that I was already dead,
>
> I would have mourned
>
> my loss of life.

**About the Illustrations**

# About the Illustrations

The interplay between ink painting and Zen Buddhism originated in China and migrated to Japan. During Japan's feudal period, Zen style ink painting became a mode of spiritual expression for many samurai. Certainly, this association was not universal. Not all samurai were Zen adherents and not all samurai possessed a predisposition for artistic talent. Readers interested in some examples of the synergy between Zen Buddhism, painting, and the samurai should refer to *A Book of Five Rings: The Classic Guide to Strategy* and *The Sword of No-Sword: Life of Master Warrior Tesshu* (see Bibliography.)

There are several style points that distinguish Zen schools of ink painting. The most apparent is that the paintings are monochrome, typically painted with black ink on a rice paper.

The composition of the painting demonstrates the aesthetic values of directness and simplicity. The composition of the painting is reduced to its minimal essential form, without ornamentation, elaboration, or refinement.

Another aesthetic characteristic of the composition is that it communicates a sense of isolation around the painting's subject. This tension is resolved as the observer interacts with the painting. The tension and resolution combine to create a sense of completeness.

Often the subjects of these paintings are drawn from a standard repertory of Zen themes. It is not the intent of the artist to create a detailed copy of a previous rendering. With Zen painting, the concept of original and copy is immaterial. Each artist's rendition is a completely personal statement that stands on its own. The artists may also select new subjects of their own choice. Often, a painting's subject matter will appear to be trivial or humorous; however, something serious always lurks beneath the surface.

# Zen Stories of the Samurai

Finally, the actual process of painting requires both the skill of a swordsman and a Zen attitude on the part of the artist. The rice paper is very porous and has a characteristic of "bleeding" when the brush is left in one spot for more than an instant. The ink is indelible and there is no possibility to rework an erroneous brush stroke. The act of painting is direct and quick. The brush moves swiftly, seldom leaving the paper and making as few strokes as possible.

## Cover: Monk Writing

The monk appears to be reflecting on his brief composition of the character *man*. In Zen, parsimony is an asset in communicating the truth. Zen Master Bankei often said that in his experience, teaching people simply meant dealing with them in their present moment. Bringing in additional talk of scripture, masters, saints, or Buddha was superfluous (see *Bankei Zen* in the Bibliography).

## Chapter 1: Bodai Daruma

Bodai Daruma is considered the patriarch of Zen Buddhism. He left behind no likeness, but in Zen painting, he is readily recognized by his stern expression, beard, and single brushstroke robe. He is often portrayed with elongated ears and an earring.

In Zen, many references to Bodai Daruma are metaphorical. References of Bodai Daruma's missionary trip from India to China are used to represent the progress of Zen adherents from novice state to enlightenment. The Zen expression, "The man (Bodai Daruma) from the East (India) has no beard" is an apparent contradiction. The beard is one of the signatures by which images of Bodai Daruma are easily recognized. This quotation is used as a caution or rebuke against discriminating or dualistic thinking.

## About the Illustrations

### Chapter 2: Hotei and Butterfly

Hotei is the wandering monk. In Zen art, Hotei is typically depicted as a rotund, jovial monk with a walking staff and a large sack. Hotei is associated with happiness and good fortune. He is a patron of children. Zen paintings often capture Hotei as he momentarily stops his wandering and takes in a lesson from nature. In this painting, Hotei leans on his sack, propped up on his elbows while he contemplates a butterfly.

### Chapter 3: Laughing Hotei

Hotei's large belly and large sack superficially suggest a problem. The traveling monk begs for food, yet Hotei does not appear to have missed a meal. He travels without possessions, yet his sack is unusually large. These features are metaphorical references to the richness of the spiritual message that Hotei brings. Hotei's laugh shakes the very ground as it reflects the simplicity of Zen enlightenment.

### Chapter 4: Monk Sleeping on Tiger

The monk appears to be resting peacefully. Has he fallen victim to a delusion of safety that will destroy him when the tiger awakens? If the monk has no fear, can he be the tiger's prey? If the monk has no aggression, can he be the tiger's enemy?

### Chapter 5: Moon, Reflection, and Monkey Artist

In the early days of Zen, high quality mirrors were not commonly available. The image of a full moon shining in a still body of water was one of the few examples of a flawless reflection. For Zen practitioners, the image of a moon reflection is a metaphor for a calm mind that has no discriminating thoughts and does not distort the true image of reality.

In Zen art, this metaphor is often reinforced by the inclusion of a monkey. The propensity for monkeys to mimic behaviors without

**Zen Stories of the Samurai**

understanding them is symbolic of the actions of the unenlightened as they stumble through life.

Typically, a monkey can see both the moon in the sky and its identical reflection in the water. While a monkey cannot reach the moon in the sky, it can reach the moon's image in the water. However, the very act of touching the reflection in the water would distort and destroy the reflection.

In this rendition, the monkey is not reaching for the reflected moon. The monkey has become the artist. Note that the monkey is painting the moon after having painted the reflection and that we, the viewers, have no direct view of the moon itself.

## Chapter 6:  Demon Meditating

Even a demon, if he changes his thinking and devotes himself to meditation, can become a Buddha.

## Chapter 7: Monk Ripping Scripture

A clergyman ripping up a copy of the scripture would likely be considered sacrilegious. That the clergyman would be laughing while committing this outrage might be taken as a sign of madness. Yet this painting is consistent with the Zen saying: "If you meet the Buddha, kill him!" At some point in our spiritual development, we can progress to the level of spiritual adulthood. At this point, over attachment to our teachers and their teaching methods can become an impediment to fulfilling our spiritual responsibilities. These attachments become as ludicrous and dysfunctional as training wheels on a racing bicycle.

## Back Cover

The early Buddhist monks in India supported themselves entirely by begging for alms. As Buddhism spread to China and Japan, this practice was modified due to climate, monastic architecture, and social factors. Zen monks in feudal Japan practiced a stylized form of begging where they periodically left the monastery, traveling as

## About the Illustrations

a group, to beg in the nearby towns. The traditional straw hat and straw raincoats worn by the monks provide silhouettes that are reminiscent of mushrooms. As a group of monks walked through a town, they chanted and assumed a confident stance with their staffs, signifying that there is nothing weak or ignoble about religious mendicancy. This begging exercise served to remind the monks of the strict, original Buddhist monastic rules. It also gave lay people a chance to exercise charity and earn spiritual merit.

# About the Authors

### Author

**Neal Dunnigan** holds the rank of 3rd dan in Aikido and has studied martial arts with noted Japanese and American instructors for over three decades. While traveling as a technology architect for major corporations, Neal has trained and served as guest instructor in dojos across the United States. Dunnigan resides in Kingfisher, Oklahoma.

### Illustrator

**John Hrabushi** has disciplined his life around Zen, art, and martial arts. A long time student of Zen, he is also an accomplished professional artist, specializing in oriental watercolor painting. A martial arts practitioner and instructor, he holds the rank of 4th dan in Aikido. He resides in New Haven, Connecticut.

Neal and John began their study of martial arts together over 30 years ago.

### Foreword

**Lorraine DiAnne** holds the rank of 6th dan and title of Shihan (master teacher) in Aikido and holds the rank of 6th dan in Iaido. She is a member of the U.S. Aikido Federation – Western Region where she has held several leadership positions. DiAnne Sensei was featured in *Women in Aikido* by Andrea Siegel (North Atlantic Books, 1993). DiAnne Sensei operates the West Side Aikido dojo in West Springfield, Massachusetts and frequently teaches at seminars across the Unites States and abroad.

# Bibliography

Bellah, Robert. *Tokugawa Religion: The Values of Pre-Industrial Japan*. Boston: The Free Press, 1957. Reprint. Boston: Beacon Press, 1970.

Craig, Darrell. *Iai: The Art of Drawing the Sword*. Darrell Craig, 1981. Reprint. Rutland, Vermont: Charles E. Tuttle, 1993.

Deshimaru, Taisen. *The Zen Way to the Martial Arts*. New York: E. P. Dutton, 1982.

Friday, Karl, and Seki Humitake. *Legacies of the Sword: The Kashima-Shinryu and the Samurai Martial Culture*. Honolulu: University of Hawaii Press, 1997.

Gluck, Jay. *Zen Combat*. Jay Gluk, 1962. Reprint. New York: Ballantine Books, 1976.

Haskel, Peter. *Bankei Zen: Translations from the Record of Bankei*. Peter Haskel and Yoshito Hakeda, 1984. Reprint. New York: Grove Weidenfeld, 1989.

Herrigel, Eugen. *Zen in the Art of Archery*. New York: Pantheon Books, 1953. Reprint. New York: Vintage Books, 1971.

Hoffmann, Yoel. *Japanese Death Poems: Written by Zen Monks and Haiku Poets on the Verge of Death*. Rutland, Vermont: Charles E. Tuttle, 1986. Reprint. 1990.

Holmes, Stewart, and Chimyo Horioka. *Zen Art for Meditation*. Rutland, Vermont: Charles E. Tuttle, 1973. Reprint. 1982.

Hyams, Joe. *Zen in the Martial Arts*. Los Angeles: J. P. Tarcher, 1979.

Kamata, Shigeo, and Kenji Shimizu. *Zen and Aikido*. Originally published in Japanese as *Zen to Aikido*. Reprint in English. Tokyo: Aiki News, 1992.

Kapleau, Phillip. The *Three Pillars of Zen; Teaching, Practice, and Enlightenment*. Garden City, New Jersey: Doubleday, 1980.

Kammer, Reinhard. *The Way of the Sword*. Munich: Otto-Wilhelm-Barth Verlag, 1969. Reprint in English. Boston: Arkana, 1986.

Kushner, Kenneth. *One Arrow, One Life: Zen, Archery, and Daily Life*. New York: Arkana, 1988.

Leggett, Trevor. *The Warrior Koans: Early Zen in Japan*. Boston: Arkana, 1985.

_____. *Zen and the Ways*. Boulder: Shambhala, 1978.

## Zen Stories of the Samurai

Merton, Thomas. *Mystics and Zen Masters*. Trappist, Kentucky: The Abbey of Gethsemani, 1961. Reprint. New York: Farrar, Straus, and Giroux, 1999.

Musashi, Miyamoto. *A Book of Five Rings: The Classic Guide to Strategy*. Translator: Victor Harris, 1974. Reprint. Woodstock, New York: Overlook Press, 1982.

Nitobe, Inazo. *Bushido: The Warrior's Code*. New York: G. P. Putnam's Sons, 1905. Reprint. Burbank, California: Ohara, 1979.

Onuma, Hideharu. *Kyudo: The Essence and Practice of Japanese Archery*. New York: Kodansha, 1993.

Ratti, Oscar, and Adele Westbrook. *Secrets of the Samurai: A Survey of the Martial Arts of Feudal Japan*. Rutland, Vermont: Charles E. Tuttle, 1973. Reprint. Edison, New Jersey: Castle Books, 1999.

Reps, Paul. *Zen Flesh, Zen Bones: A Collection of Zen and Pre-Zen Writings*. Garden City, New Jersey: Anchor Books, 1961.

Ross, Nancy. *The World of Zen: An East-West Anthology*. New York: Vintage, 1960.

Sato, Hiroaki. *The Sword and the Mind*. Woodstock, New York: The Overlook Press, 1986.

Soho, Takuan. *The Unfettered Mind: Writings of the Zen Master to the Sword Master*. New York: Kodansha, 1986. Reprint. 1987.

Stevens, *John. Budo Secrets: Teachings of the Martial Arts Masters*. Boston: Shambhala, 2001.

_____. *The Sword of No-Sword: Life of the Master Warrior Tesshu*. Boston: Shambhala, 1984. Revised. 1989.

Storry, Richard. *The Way of the Samurai*. New York: G. P. Putnam's Sons, 1978.

Stryk, Lucian, and Takashi Ikemoto. *The Penguin Book of Zen Poetry*. London: Allen Lane, 1977. Reprint. New York: Penguin Books, 1981.

Suzuki, Daisetz T. *The Awaking of Zen*. Boulder, Colorado: Prajna Press, 1980. Reprint. Boston: Shambhala, 2000.

_____. *Zen and Japanese Culture*. New York: Bollingen Foundation, 1959. Reprint. 1973.

Suzuki, Shunryu. *Zen Mind, Beginner's Mind*. New York: Weatherhill, 1973.

Turnbull, Stephen. *Samurai Warriors*. New York: Blandford Press, 1987.

## Bibliography

Tsunetomo, Yamamoto, and William Wilson. *Hagakure: The Book of the Samurai*. New York: Kodansha, 1979. Reprint. New York: Avon Books, 1981.

Warner, Gordon, and Donn Draeger. *Japanese Swordsmanship: Technique and Practice*. New York: Weatherhill, 1982 Reprint. 1990.

Wilson, William. *Budoshoshinshu: The Warrior's Primer of Daidoji Yuzan*. Burbank, California: Ohara, 1984.

_____. *Ideals of the Samurai: Writings of Japanese Warriors*. Burbank, Calafornia: Ohara, 1982.

# Zen Stories of the Samurai

# Index

Archery, 21, 47

Bankei, 53, 54, 55, 110, 125, 130
Banzo, 31, 32, 33
boat, 107, 109
Bodai Daruma, 21, 29, 58, 92, 125
Buddha, 57, 63, 72, 99, 125, 127
Bukko Kokushi, 82

cherry blossoms, 43
concentration, 43, 57, 115, 116
Confucius, 54
cowardice, 59

demon, 68, 77
Diamond King, 77
Diamond Sutra, 119
discriminating mind, 59, 63
duel, 114, 115, 116, 120, 121, 122
duty, 24, 49

fan, 53, 96, 98
fear, 26, 82, 111, 116, 126
fencing, 21, 27, 31, 34, 35, 36, 37, 45, 46, 53, 55, 60, 61, 62, 63, 65, 97, 103, 107, 108, 114, 115, 121, 122
fly chaser, 63

garden, 43, 44, 85, 86, 97
Great Vow, 74

Hakuin, 65, 66
Heaven, 66, 78, 79
Hojo Takatoki, 78
Hojo Tokimune, 82
Hojo Tokiyori, 68
honor, 24, 46, 116, 120
horse, 57, 58, 63, 103, 104
Hotei, 41, 51, 126

Ichigen, 71

Jizo, 68, 71, 72, 74, 75

Kagetoki Kajiwara, 69
Kato, 48, 49, 50
Kawanakajima, 95
Kenchoji, 68, 69, 70, 71, 72, 74, 76, 78, 79
Korea, 22, 83, 97
Korinji, 53

Lake Biwa, 107
loyalty, 24, 76, 77

Mamiya Munekatsu, 74
Masamune, 87, 88
Matajuro, 31, 32, 33
meditation, 20, 21, 43, 57, 83, 127
monkey, 101, 102, 126, 127
moon, 126, 127
morning glories, 85, 86

Nitta Sadayoshi, 71
Nobunaga, 85
Nobushige, 65, 66

Ota Dokan, 123
Ouchi Yoshitaka, 119

page of Munenori, 43, 44
pillow, 37, 38
poetry, 21, 28, 47, 119, 123
puzzle, 71, 74

Rankei, 68, 69
Rankei Doryu, 68
riddle, 71, 74
Riko, 89, 90, 91
Rinan, 87, 88

Sakawa Koresda, 72
salt, 94
Segaki, 69, 70
Sen no Rikyu, 48, 85
Setsubun, 68

133

# Index

Shogun, xvii, 23, 45, 68, 69, 81, 82, 83, 84, 85, 97, 98, 99, 100, 101, 102, 103, 113
Shoju Ronin, 60
Sozan, 78, 79
stick, 33, 101
suicide, 26, 119
Suwa Bunkuro, 103

Tadamasa, 78, 79
Taiko, 48
Takeda Shingen, 94
Takuan Soho, 27, 97, 101
Tea Master, 48, 85
Tetsugyu, 59
tiger, 97, 98, 99, 100, 126
Toden, 76, 77
Tokugawa Iyemitsu, 45, 97, 101, 103

Toyotomi Hideyoshi, 85
Tsukahara Bokuden, 37, 107
tunnel, 39, 40

Uesugi Kenshin, xvi, 92, 94

Yagyu Munenori, 27, 28, 31, 43, 45, 97, 101, 103
Yakkoku, 74
Yakusan, 89, 90
Yama no Uchi, 113
Yamamoto Gorozaemon, 59
Yamana Morofuyu, 57
Yamoaka Tesshu, 35
Yekiwo, 92, 93
Yoritomo Minamoto, 69
Yoriyasu, 76, 77

Zenkai, 39, 40

**Zen Stories of the Samurai**

## About the Font

The font used in *Zen Stories of the Samurai* is Verdana, created in 1996 by master British designer Matthew Carter. It is ubiquitous on the Internet due to its simplicity and legibility on a computer screen. It is also highly readable in print media. Verdana was selected for ease on the eye, which should help the reader enjoy returning to these Zen stories again and again.

CPSIA information can be obtained at www.ICGtesting.com
224094LV00001B/17/P